Unscrambled Thoughts

A Poetic Journey

EDEANA FERNANDES

INDIA · SINGAPORE · MALAYSIA

ISBN   979-8-89277-577-9

To my family and friends, thank you for believing in me

To every reader who picked up this book, for giving my words a chance, and to those who finds a piece of themselves within these poems.

Contents

1.	Call You Mine	9
2.	I Choose You	10
3.	Superhero	11
4.	Some Things Are Meant To Be	12
5.	Some Things Are Meant To Be – II	13
6.	Naked	14
7.	It's Ok Not To Be Ok	15
8.	You Are Always On My Mind	16
9.	I Want To Feel Free	17
10.	Us Against The World	18
11.	Silent Screams	19
12.	Don't Let Me Go	20
13.	Say Something	21
14.	C'est La Vie (This Is Life)	22
15.	Thinking Out Loud	23
16.	Second Chance	24
17.	All Of The Stars	25
18.	Nostalgia	26
19.	Escape	27
20.	Trapped	28
21.	The Guardian	29
22.	Lost In The Ruins	30
23.	Are You There?	31
24.	Moment Of Truth	32
25.	Photograph	33
26.	A Bend In The Road	34
27.	You And I	35
28.	Safe House	36

29. A Wishful Heart   37

30. A Chapter From The Past   38

31. Remember When   39

32. So They Said   40

33. Trail Of Thoughts   41

34. Not Knowing   42

35. Start Of Something New   43

36. Memory   44

37. A Promise   45

38. Epilogue   46

39. Guardian Angel   47

40. You Are Only Human   48

41. Here I Am   49

42. Now Or Never   50

43. Survivor   51

44. Quarantine   52

45. Euphoria   53

46. Written In The Stars   54

47. To The Children Of Tomorrow   55

48. Aloha...!   56

49. Unscrambled Thoughts   57

50. I Will Always Love You   50

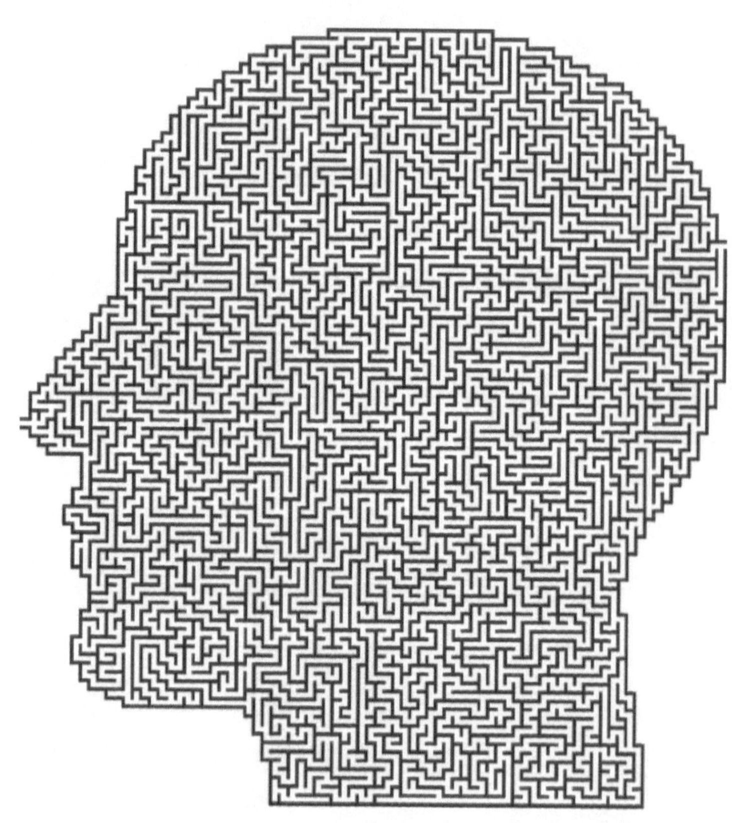

1. CALL YOU MINE

Has anyone told you lately,
How perfect of a human you are.
That every essence of you is kind and pure.
That God took His time creating you.
How lucky am I, to call you mine!

Have you ever been told,
That there is just one edition of you.
That there is truly none like you.
That you are irreplaceable.
How wonderful it is, to call you mine!

Why hasn't someone told you this,
How wonderful of a person you are.
That you're amazing just as you are,
Out of 7.9 billion people in this world
How grateful I am, to call you mine!

Has anyone ever said to you,
That YOU are worth keeping?
That through all highs and lows,
You are worth holding on to.
And I'm blessed to call you mine!

You're my once in a lifetime.
You're my fairytale come true.
You're my miracle in flesh and blood.
Even though reality now feels like a dream
Blissfully aware that I get to call you mine!

2. I CHOOSE YOU

Today I choose you
Just as I did yesterday
Or the day before that
Or the very first day we met

Today I choose you,
To be my go-to person
And when I'm falling
To help me break that fall

Today I choose you
To be my listening ear
When I'm fighting with myself
To be my counsel and advocate

Today I choose you
To be my mirror my reflection
When I say or do wrong
To gently show me my flaws

I choose you today
Without a shadow of fear or doubt
I will always choose you
Every time for the rest of my life.

3. SUPERHERO

I hope that someday you will know
When you look in the mirror,
That your scars don't matter,
That you are beautiful enough.

I hope that someday you will know
When you decide to walk around,
That you don't have to hide anymore,
That you are imperfectly perfect.

I hope that someday you will know
When you go out with loved ones
That your wallet size doesn't matter
That it's the memories made that counts.

I hope that someday you will know
When you fall prey to prejudice
That no matter what the world may say
That you are who you choose to be.

I hope that you always know your worth
That you are enough, you are loved.
That you are strong, you are mighty
That you are your own superhero.

4. SOME THINGS ARE MEANT TO BE

Oh, we were different.
Not like day and night,
Or like north and south.
There was a lot not in common.

Our thoughts barely matched.
But we'd talk over drinks we enjoyed,
Or movies we both equally liked
Yet we were different from each other.

Sometimes when I think about us,
I get lost in deep wonder.
Trying to figure out one small question,
How did we end up together like this?

Opposites attract was just a saying,
Up until now that I felt it myself.
There is something about him
He's not like the others I've known

I find comfort as I sit close to him
My head resting against his chest.
Our fingers intertwined with each other
Maybe some things are simply meant to be.

5. SOME THINGS ARE MEANT TO BE – II

The day is finally here today
The one we had been waiting for
The day we had been dreaming of
The day we will always remember.

As I stood there waiting for you,
I couldn't help but feel nervous
Breathe, just breathe I told myself
You've prepared well for this day

As the moment drew nearer
I couldn't wait to see you now
I could feel my soul calming down.
You were there at the end of the aisle

They said we were different
They said our worlds collide
You're everything I am not
That's what makes me whole

With each step you took towards me
I felt our differences unite.
No matter what the world says,
Darling some things are meant to be.

6. NAKED

Hey, are you there?
I'm standing here, can you see me?
I'm ready to go to the next level
Leaving all my fears far behind

I'm standing here without a drop of pride
Cause I really don't want to mess it up.
I'm standing here because you care.
Here I am, wearing my heart on my sleeve.

This mask I wear has to come off now,
No more fights, I can't do this anymore.
You've given me more than I asked.
I'm here now giving more than I ever can.

If you could please stay with me
You got to wait now that I'm done
I don't need anyone, I just need you.
I can't pretend that I don't need you

Here I stand before you in surrender
I'm standing here making it clear
I'm ready to break down these walls
Cause I'm standing here naked.

7. IT'S OK NOT TO BE OK

It's a tough world out there
Maybe even a complicated world
The more and more we get to know
The more twisted the knots get

It's a frightful world out there
Maybe even an unforgiving world
The lonelier you get
The more it drives you crazy

It's a complex world out there
Maybe even a more intense world
The more inventions were made
The more damage had to be controlled

The world is not a simple place
Maybe not as bad as it seems
Maybe it's yet to find its peace
Maybe it's yet to settle down

The world is vast and unending
Maybe that's why it's ok we get lost
Maybe it's alright we don't understand
It's alright we don't have to know it all.

8. YOU ARE ALWAYS ON MY MIND

I think about you
Every time I hear a song
When I listen to the lyrics
And I feel the words and beats

I think about you
Every time I read a book
When I envision the scene
And I picture us in that story

I think about you
Every time I watch a movie
When the boy meets his girl
And they have a happily ever after

I think about you
Every time I close my eyes
My thoughts wander to fond times
And I feel peaceful and happy

I think about you all the time
You're constantly on my mind.
The longer I am away from you
The more I long to be with you

9. I WANT TO FEEL FREE

A strange Monday morning
A new week, a new day had begun
A strange day, a strange feeling
This time no new promises were made

I spent the whole day thinking
Lost in a dark and blank wonder
I didn't feel like myself that day
Something was definitely missing

I was present in that crowded room
I smiled and greeted everyone
My day seemed to be on auto pilot
I was in control and yet slipping away

I've never been like this before
Distant from my own self,
Would I ever feel whole again?
If only I knew what was missing.

I needed to get my life on track
Take the wheels, steer steadily
This is what I must do right now
I want to feel free; I want to feel free.

10. US AGAINST THE WORLD

If I could tell the world one thing.
I'd tell how much I love You
I'd write it on every wall I can
And put it in all the papers.

But you won't let me tell it all
Not a whisper to a single soul
For you think a lot and fear a lot
you worry what the world would say

If I could change one thing,
I'd change this wicked society
Their condemned unfair conditions
And their vicious thoughts

But there's nothing I can do,
They won't ever stop talking
I'd break their rules to prove them wrong,
But they don't matter to me as much as you.

If I could tell you one thing,
I'd tell you every single wish I've mad.
From 11:11 to fallen lashes to shooting stars
All the silent prayers I've made for us.

But I believe in miracles and in us
And that today I have you with me
In a world that would tear us apart
I'd do it all to keep us bound together.

11. SILENT SCREAMS

Hello? Is anyone out there?
I'm calling out to you
Can you hear my whispers?
Will you reach for me?

This chaotic noise in my head
Get it out, get it out!
I need to think straight
Can you help me find peace?

I have fallen, fallen very hard
In this dark black hole
All this negativity holding me down
Take my hand, help me out.

I hear what their eyes talk
I can hear them all the time
They stare as if they know it all
Make them stop, make them stop

My thoughts turn to nightmare
I'm slowly steadily giving up
If only someone could hear me
If only they heard my silent screams.

12. DON'T LET ME GO

Someday I will be gone
Gone away from your reach
Maybe to another country
Or perhaps to another world

Someday you may look for me
And I won't be around anymore
You would want to hear me
But the old videos never be enough.

Someday you will feel this distance
And you'd want to get closer
No matter how much you travel
The gap never seems to fill

Someday you will wish I were around
Just like the good old times
You'd promise to do things differently
That we'll make things work.

Don't wait for that someday
Hold me close never let me go
Say it before it's too late
The time is now, the time is now.

13. SAY SOMETHING

Say something that,
Will make my day.
That will be my thoughts,
That will make me smile.

Say something that
Will take my worries far away
No matter how dark the clouds get,
Your words would be my ray of sunshine.

Say something that
Will change my world.
That no matter how hard I fall,
I'll always find the courage to get up.

Say something say anything,
Cause words can work wonders.
In times of struggles and chaos,
You will always be my saving grace.

14. C'EST LA VIE
(THIS IS LIFE)

I stumbled upon some pictures
Kept safe from dust and rust
Just as I picked up a snapshot
Memories came flooding back

I gathered up the scattered album
And sat in the comfortable corner
I recollected names almost forgotten
An involuntary smile appears

A sudden realization dawn upon
As my smile fades into a frown
Those days were some of the best
How did it all change so fast

When did it all slip far away?
When did I embrace solitude?
When did the ones I cared about?
Cause me to feel like an outcast

Tough times don't last too long
Not everyone can stick around
Except the ones who matter most
This is life, C'est la vie.

15. THINKING OUT LOUD

Do you ever think about me?
When time slows down,
When your day is gloomy
And nothing feels right.

Do you ever think of me?
When you are the happiest
When you're on top of the world
And nothing can bring you down.

Do you ever think of me?
When your mind is filled with thoughts.
Thoughts troublesome and untold
And you feel lost and alone.

Do you ever think of me?
When you count your blessings
When you look for hope and peace
And a new beginning awaits you.

When you think of me
Close your eyes and remember me
Whisper my name or call it out loud
Darling I promise, I'll be there.

16. SECOND CHANCE

"Hey wait! You can't quit."
I heard a voice behind me
I looked over my shoulder
I didn't see anyone around

I stood alone at the edge of the world
The breeze was stronger today
I watched the people hustle and bustle
I couldn't hear the traffic from up hear

The noise in my head grew louder
Mocking the debris of my dreams
Would it make a difference at all?
One less in a world of a billion?

This time I would take the plunge
I wanted to feel free and weightless
It would all end once I reached the ground
The taunting faces would fade away

"Stop where you are, don't quit!"
I heard the voice again loud and clear
On every dark cloud there's a silver lining
Look not on what's lost but what you have.

You may be in troubled waters now
But at the end of it is a beautiful horizon
You're stronger than you think
Come on, it's time to go home."

17. ALL OF THE STARS

The night had made it closer to dusk
I should sleep now, I told myself
Yet I could not stop my mind
From wandering every now and then

Staying away from you isn't easy
I now dislike this distance between us
The stars danced around the moon
I wish you were by my side holding me close.

Unlike most nights this was different
I was no longer overthinking
The sweet memories of yesterday
Were now keeping me awake.

I looked at the beautiful night sky
And replayed every memory in my head
My heart still skipped a beat or two
Never have I felt so peaceful.

I saw a shooting star that night
I never believed in making a wish before
I close my eyes and crossed my fingers
And all I could think of was you.

18. NOSTALGIA

I miss you sometimes
I miss that smile a lot
The way it worked wonders
The joy it brought to others

I miss you a lot sometimes
I miss the way you loved to stand out
How the world never bothered you
How you would mingle and blend in

I think of you every now and then
And I catch myself smiling sometimes
This feeling of nostalgia won't go away
Frankly I can't seem to do anything about it

I look at your pictures, the ones I could find
You've changed a lot over time
The one's who always said, "stay the same"
Were now the reason for you to be this way

Memories, they ever change,
Nor do they let go that easily.
I miss you every time I look back
For you exist only in my head now.

19. ESCAPE

I have always felt drawn to the sea,
The sound of the sea never failed to soothe me
The cool winds that made my hair dance
Always seemed to calm my soul

It was the quietness that I enjoyed the most
Being there by myself was magical
Most people who assumed I was lonely
Failed to see how my troubles were put to rest

There seems to be a voice that binds me
A voice so sweet I feel drawn instantly.
It's among the whispers of the trees
It's among the roars of the waves

It is here I feel safe and protected
Locked away from thoughts unpleasant
Far away from chaos and battles
This is my getaway, this is my escape.

20. TRAPPED

Hey, are you out there?
Can you hear me calling you?
I'm knocking on this door between us
My hands have begun to ache.

Is my voice reaching out to you?
Over here! if you could get me out.
Why won't you look at me?
I'm screaming my lungs out...

I have heard your demons scream
Your eyes have grown weary and dry
Your mind has wandered to a distant memory
While you are standing here before me

They see you smile, that joy in your eyes
They see you standing tall and strong
I can feel your soul in distress
Why won't you speak your heart out?

This world, what has it done to you?
How do you hide your trembling knees?
How will you hide that darkness from me?
How will you hide yourself from your own reflection?

21. THE GUARDIAN

I didn't ask him
To leave his family behind.
He did it with his head held high
It was his choice he said.

I didn't ask him
For the sacrifice he had to make
He did it, without a single complain
For him it was about the service.

He didn't have to do it,
Staying up all night, no rest at all
It was his decision, he couldn't go back now
His priorities were different now

He didn't want to be back home
Yet here he was, his life hanging by a thread
Truth be told, I didn't know him at all,
Yet I felt compelled to stay by his side

I watched him win his fight over death
Waited patiently for his eyes to adjust
I couldn't stop myself for asking him, "why?"
"I promised my mother I'd protect her" he
whispered.

22. LOST IN THE RUINS

She held on to her doll tightly
As she rummaged through the debris
Her hands were too small and weak
Yet she didn't stop her search

She crawled underneath the fallen wall
Of the house her father had envisioned.
She struggled to get a clear sight
The smoke hadn't cleared yet

Where was it? She thought to herself...
She was desperate to find it...
That toy her infant brother loved
It was the only way to soothe him

She finally found it tossed in the corner
She tried to reach for it but failed...
She quickly got to her feet
Dusted herself and ran to her mother

She tried to wake her but she was still
In that moment she knew it all
She rocked her brother to sleep
As she sang the only lullaby she knew.

23. ARE YOU THERE?

I lost a part of me today
This time I didn't bother.
I've grown tired, very tired
Of picking up the pieces.

How many times could I do that?
Put myself together again.
When I know for certain,
That I'd fall apart yet again

I've grown weary of that mask,
I can't pretend anymore
Put on that smile and fool the world
No, I have lost the strength for that

How much more should I forgive?
How much more should I forget?
For once I don't want to do any of it.
Would it then make a difference?

This time can I think about myself?
Would you come and hold me?
Would you be the one to console me?
Are you there for me like I am for you?

24. MOMENT OF TRUTH

How much do you love me? He asked.
He held my hands and looked into my eyes,
As if searching for the answer.
How much do you care?

I could not move, let alone speak
He's eyes were fixed on mine
The more he looked the more I drowned
As if he put me in a hypnotic trance.

He asked again, one more time
I wanted to tell him, answer him
But then what could I say?
How was I supposed to quantify my love?

I let him speak every time we met.
And watched his expression change
I could see he's eyes sparkle with excitement
But today was different, it was my turn to speak.

"I love you, twice as much as the stars in the sky,
From dusk to dawn, you're always on my mind.
You've changed my life the day we met,
And today I can't imagine not loving you.

You're my breath of fresh air,
You bring me the peace I long for.
You're my escape from the real world
Now you tell me, how much do you love me?"

25. PHOTOGRAPH

He was almost certain now,
She was the one his life lacked.
Yes, he could feel it now,
She was the one who completed him

He could simply look at her,
And he knew he felt happiness.
Her hair, her eyes, her smile,
God did take his time creating her.

He longed to see her, meet her,
Just one glimpse of her that's all
He felt his world brighten up
She was his world after all

He was going to tell her, it was time
He looked into her eyes and confessed
But she didn't say anything, just smiled
He didn't mind that, her lips had his attention.

Oh, how he wished she'd say something
Perhaps a few words of love
He closed his eyes and took a deep breath
As he placed her photograph alongside his own.

26. A BEND IN THE ROAD

He still remembered that day,
When he saw her for the first time.
He remembered the way she talked
And smiled, even the dress she wore that night.

It didn't matter at that time,
It was just another ordinary day
But today, months later he reminisced
And found himself smiling thinking about her

He recalled that night they met
When his lips touched hers.
He finally felt what it was like
To be kissed by an angel.

He found himself longing for her,
Just the sight of her would suffice.
Oh, how he loved the sound of her laughter
Or the way her eyes would shine.

Somehow he evaded the bitter truth,
She was the moon, he was her wolverine
No matter how much he loved her
Would she ever be his?

27. YOU AND I

He paced up and down the hall way
Checking his watch for the 10th time
He was growing impatient,
But the wait was a must.
He checked himself in the mirror
Straightened his tie and tucked his shirt.

She tossed her dress on the bed
And tried on her 5th outfit already
The earrings matched perfectly this time
Her make-up was finally right
Her hair, thank God it stayed the way she wanted
She took a deep breath as she watched herself

What was taking her so long
No, they weren't going to be late
He made sure of it while making reservations
That was their favorite place after all
This had to be the perfect evening.

She finally walked out of the room
Completely satisfied with her looks
She felt a fluster in her stomach
She saw him at the end of the stairs
And felt a wave of tranquility
The wait was perfect for the perfect evening

He watched her talk and then eat
Oh God help him, she was beautiful.
She watched him, his eyes full of love
Lord help her, he was perfect.
He held her hand in his, the ring was just right
Her hand fit in his perfect, she had to say yes.
They were meant for each other.

28. SAFE HOUSE

Wait a while and stay with me,
Let's sit by the bonfire, swaying to our tune.
Let's hear the waves crashing in the distant,
And watch the clouds uncover the starry night.

Hold my hand and stay a while with me,
If you thought sunsets were beautiful,
Let me show you breathtaking sunrises.
Let's see the stars disappear into sunlight.

Sit by my side let's slow time down.
Let me look into your eyes, our fingers intertwined.
Let the whole world around us fade away.
And for a while, just for a while it's just me and you.

Stay a while and celebrate with me.
Let's lead each other through a dance or two.
Let's wrap our arms around each other.
Just you and me, in perfect synchrony.

Walk with me by my side, let's journey together.
Let's embark the path that waits for us.
If the times get rough let me be your rock.
And from all troubles, I'll be your safe house.

29. A WISHFUL HEART

It was one of those long walks
Down the memory lane so clear
The fun, the stress, the never-ending talks,
Were some of the things truly familiar

There were a few wrong turns
Turns never to be taken
The ones that I should have ignored
But my path somehow led me there.

If life gave me a second chance
Would I still walk the same road?
Would things change for the better?
Would this change really matter?

Do such opportunities even exist?
Chances as such so hard to resist.
A chance to start it all over again.
To walk away from all remorse and pain

Life is not a game to be played
There's no restart button
The person I am, the people I met,
Is as was destined, as was planned.

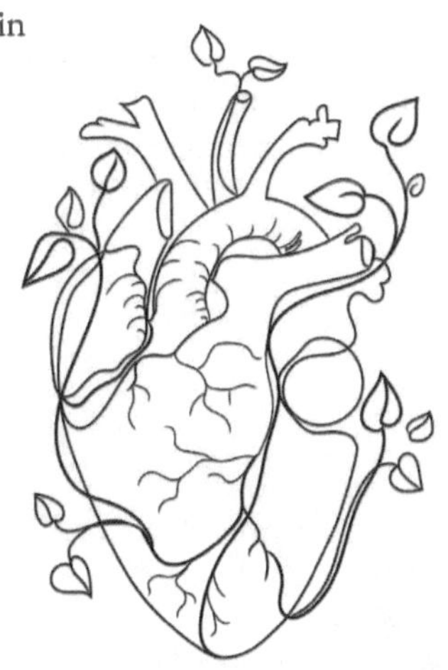

30. A CHAPTER FROM THE PAST

She said she was done
And began walking towards the sea.
In that moment she felt a pain
She could not describe.
The sound of the sea
The view of the sunset was meant to soothe
This was her sense of comfort after all.
But on this day, it didn't,
Instead, it brought back memories,
Of the numerous sunsets watched together.
Breathe, they said breathe and let go
But how was she to breathe?
When he took her breath away?
How was she to let go?
No, she made up her mind.
She would get up and move on
She had her whole life ahead of her.
She had a family that loved her
And her friends who needed her
This was all that mattered nothing else.

31. REMEMBER WHEN

I remember it all
I remember the day we met
It was the best day of my life.
I remember the sound of your voice
And the feel of your touch.

I remember, I remember it all
The night I woke up terrified
And you soothed me to sleep
I remember you just being there
When no one else was.

I remember everything
The music of your laughter
The rhythm of your heartbeat
I remember the fear in your eyes
While being strong just for me

I remember it all so well,
Every day we had, the good, the bad
Even the day we parted ways.
And I truly hope you remember me
Like I remember you.

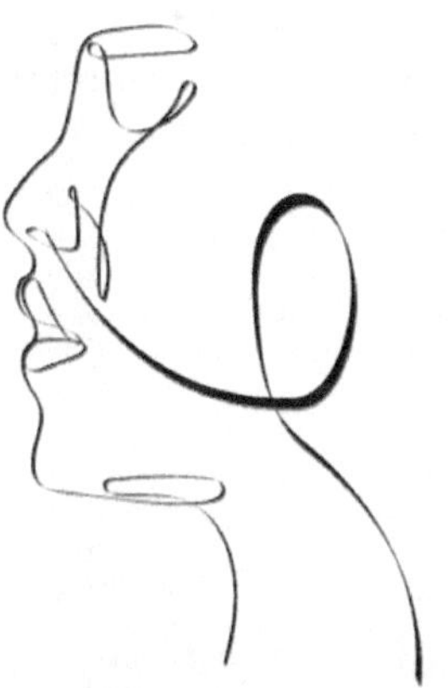

32. SO THEY SAID

They told me to start over,
It would do me good.
Leave it all behind
And never look back

They said I'd feel better
They said I would want that.
The misery of today,
Would end in time.

They said I'd be free,
Free from it all.
Free from the burden,
Free from the tears.

They told me to let it go,
It was easier way out.
They told me to move on
And never look back

I took a step back
Starred into the abyss thinking
Would they still say the same,
Had they walked a mile in my shoes?

33. TRAIL OF THOUGHTS

I walked away from the crowd
Towards a place I could be at peace
I needed some time by myself
With the quietness that I miss.

I began thinking of the past,
The times my happiness would last,
I recalled the times I simply smiled
Relived the moments my eyes never cried

I found a place dark and empty
I decided to wait a few hours.
Began hearing my thoughts out loud,
Whilst gazing at the distant stars.

I stopped and turned around to see,
The weary path that led me here
Nothing could evade what was meant to be
All that's lost is now only a memory.

Someday everything will make perfect sense.
I have fallen risen and moved on.
As reality begins to supersede pretense,
The truth of life begins to dawn.

34. NOT KNOWING

There is nothing scarier,
Than the feeling of confusion.
To be sad or make merry,
Seems to be the toughest decision.

What feels right, turns out wrong
What was the best is now just another song.
Uncertainty and doubt begin to grow,
All I need is a little help or more.

Nothing is more awful than not knowing,
Whether to hold on or keep going.
Where there are so many reasons to stay,
There seems no point to delay.

When all seems lost and nothing is right,
Look around, a loved one is always within sight
To hold you and take you through,
To guide you or simply be with you.

With a little trust and a little care
Nothing at all is worth all that scare.
With the right ones by your side,
The longest journey is worth the ride.

35. START OF SOMETHING NEW

I think of you not knowing,
The love for you from me.
I look at you not believing,
How much my heart longs to see.

I watched you smiling,
The wrinkles it gave your face.
I saw your eyes brighten and sparkle,
I watched sorrow leave without a trace.

I heard the sound of your laughter,
And I watched you in wonder.
The witty remarks that thereafter,
Got me to sit and just ponder.

I reached out for your hand,
And walked along with you.
Wished the moment would never end
This was the start of something new.

36. MEMORY

I didn't know him for long,
Yet I thought of him every time.
Every sing the radio played
Reminded me of someone who never was mine.

I didn't know him as much as others.
Yet I miss those days we spent together.
The times I would go out of my way,
I recall them every single day.

I didn't know him long enough
Yet I felt I knew him my whole life.
Being far apart now is tough
Wish I could go back in time again

I didn't know him as much as I thought
Yet he is my favorite story.
The moments that form every new chapter,
Are from a fond book I call memory.

37. A PROMISE

I saw you sit alone that day.
As I walked towards your way.
I saw your eyes in the dark glimmer,
Caused by the flow of tears.

The sight of you moved me.
Wished I could do something to set you free.
I felt completely shattered and helpless,
But all I could do was sit with you selfless.

I could not understand anything,
For you I wanted to do everything
I tried my best but could do nothing
All I wanted to do was see you smiling.

If only you could look up and see,
All the love for you from me.
That through thick and thin I'm always here,
To bring back your smile and take away your fear.

Maybe only then you'll know,
From all the fears you'll grow.
And when you'll hold on to me,
All the promised happiness you will see.

38. EPILOGUE

This year has taught me a lot.
I have learnt to be strong,
When I had no one around,
I've learnt to stand tall, stand strong.

This year has taught me a lot.
I have learnt to take that chance.
What once seemed impossible,
I've learnt to at least give it a try.

This year has taught me a lot.
I have learnt to be heard.
When my head is filled with thoughts,
I've learnt to channel my voice.

This year has taught me a lot.
I've learnt to forget and forgive.
Even though it's easier to hate,
I've learnt that to love is to live.

This year has truly taught me a lot.
This changing time has taught me a lot.
But most of all I've learnt to be myself,
And for that, just that I am grateful.

39. GUARDIAN ANGEL

As he stood there at the end of the aisle,
He had this look everyone talked about.
He had his gaze fixed at that one person,
His heartbeat synced with her footsteps.

Her long dress was white as snow,
Her hair could not be more perfect.
She looked the prettiest that day,
Like she was God's most beautiful creation.

As she stood near him at the altar,
He was one step closer to his perfect future.
His eyes were now filled with tears,
Is this what pure happiness felt like?

The time had come to exchange the vows,
Vows that would bind them together forever,
Vows that would be written on stones,
No matter what, can never be broken.

He held her hands and said,
"I promise to protect and respect you,
I promise to be your strength and support.
Through times good or bad, I'll stay by your side,
From this day on, I'll be your own guardian angel."

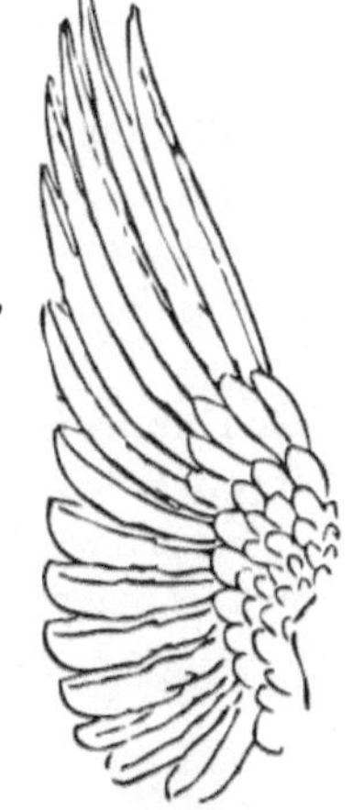

40. YOU ARE ONLY HUMAN

For the longest time I'd been an over-thinker
Locked far away in my own head
Shackled by tangled string of thoughts.
A nagging need to figure everything out.

Like a butterfly with a broken wing,
I'd wander from one broken soul to another.
Put on my cape and try rescue the damned.
How could I look past the hearts left broken?

Who's gonna save you from yourself?
A constant voice whispering coherently,
Of course, I'd ignore that, they needed me.
How else would they get out of their misery?

Only doctors save lives, said nobody ever!
Not all fires are meant to be put out by a fireman
Not all Counselors therapists, not all healers nurses.
There was that voice again but faint this time.

"You dot your I's and cross all the T's,
You make that list and check all the boxes.
Yet there you are constantly contemplating.
Heavy is the head that wears the crown.

Take a breath, it's alright to stop sometimes.
Let your feelings catch up to you for once.
Cause when you let someone break your fall,
You'll see that you are just a human too."

41. HERE I AM

If you need a listening ear
Need someone to just be there
Hear you talk your heart out
Hear you with no prejudice
Here I am, I'm reaching out.

If you ever need a shoulder
You need someone to lean on
Someone to be your strength
Or maybe even sit in silence
Look around, here I am.

If you find the world cold and empty
And you are amongst strangers
If you need a familiar face
Someone to make you feel like home
Here I am right here by your side

Here I am, always here for you
With all the love I have to give
Here I am, I'll always stand by you
Through tides, high and low,
Here I am, I'll be there for you.

42. NOW OR NEVER

Sometimes there is no next time,
No second chances, no do overs
Sometimes we get just one chance
Opportunities don't turn up again

Sometimes we meet people by chance
Some choose to stay some walk away
Sometimes we hold on to a few
These are the ones we can't live without

Sometimes life knocks us down,
We lose all faith and hope
Sometimes we feel like it's the end
There's no meaning, there's no point.

Sometimes there's no time out
Things change, people leave
What is done cannot be undone
Life does not wait for anybody

Take that leap of faith for once,
For once grab that opportunity,
And take that road less traveled
Cause sometimes, it's now or never.

43. SURVIVOR

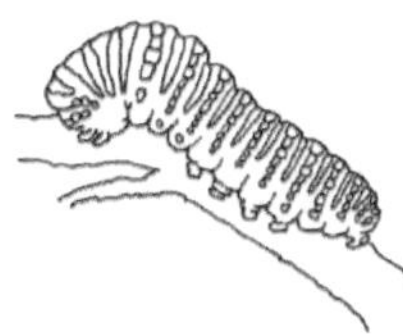

Would you have recognized me
If you met me 10 years ago?
Would you believe what you saw?
Looking at my carefree eyes?

Would you see my head held high
If you met me 5 years ago?
My shoulders squared, back straight,
Learning what it is to be an adult.

Would you see my chaotic life,
If you met me three years ago?
Drowned in work, my hair a mess
Anxiously waiting for a weekend of sleep.

Would you know my story?
If you met me today?
Would you see how far I've come?
The fights I've lost, the battles I've won.

From one's I thought were inseparable
To the ones who stood by through it all
Even though I've lost my way sometimes,
I've found myself time and time again.

As I stand staring aimlessly at the sky,
Broken yet whole, imperfect yet just right,
My wings held together by tape and glue,
I find solace in knowing that I survived.

44. QUARANTINE

Lately I've been in over my head,
Drowning in my own pool of thoughts,
Picking on smallest of the smallest issues,
Failing to understand the causality.

These walls that I built inside my head,
Is slowly, steadily closing in on me.
I'm trying, trying to push them back,
But my weary hands are not strong enough.

As the walls come crashing down,
I find myself amidst weary eyes.
Aloof and fixated on their blue screens,
Walking around just like clockwork.

I never realized how caught up I was,
Embracing the daily monotonous hustle.
Forgetting I had unresolved issues,
I had escaped from facing various truths.

This time I had nowhere else to go.
I could only run away for so long.
With the world come to an unwelcomed halt,
I now come to face my waking nightmares.

45. EUPHORIA

It truly amazes me sometimes
How often you make me smile,
How quickly you calm my nerves
How easily you make me happy.

There's something about your eyes,
Eyes that sparkle with all the love.
Even through all the pictures
You make me blush like a fool.

I sometimes stare in wonder
My life since you came along,
Somehow through all this chaos
Everything feels so meant-to-be

How do you manage to do that?
Fix my mess by just that smile.
You bring peace to my soul, joy to my eyes.
My heart beating in perfect rhythm.

How do you manage to do that?
All my troubles just go far away.
Your presence brightens my cloudy days
Adding colors in my monochromatic life

You are my best story, my fairytale
If I could ever do anything over
I'd probably meet you faster, sooner.
Cause you're worth it, you're worth it all.

46. WRITTEN IN THE STARS

My hand fits in yours like pieces of a puzzle.
Perfect as if it was just meant to be.
I look in your eyes and all I see is love,
Ever since I met you, my life feels complete.

It took me a while to understand
How so quickly we became inseparable
How so quickly you became this important.
Today I can't imagine life without you.

Thinking back I begin to realize,
Your mere presence was enough.
Enough to make me smile a lil more.
Without you trying, you made my day.

I had always been an over thinker
My mind wrapped around thoughts
Until the day you rescued me from myself
Like a lighthouse guiding me back home.

I was all out of firsts or so I thought.
From our first encounter to our first movie,
Every moment of each day a new experience.
A new meaning to happiness I finally found.

There's a sense of belongingness,
When you wrap your arms around me.
The best things in life comes unexpectedly,
And when fate intervenes magic is inevitable.

47. TO THE CHILDREN OF TOMORROW

To the children of tomorrow, I'm sorry.
I'm sorry I couldn't protect your home.
That you'll not understand nature as I did
That the air you'll breathe is not fresh anymore.

To the children of tomorrow, I'm sorry.
I'm sorry we failed to stand united.
That we let the color of our skin matter,
That we let the innocent be put to test.

To the children of tomorrow, I'm sorry.
I'm so sorry that animals are afraid of us.
That man forgot they too can feel pain.
That mankind succumbed to superiority complex.

To the children of tomorrow, fear not.
Fear not, cause some of us are still fighting.
That even though we are a small minority,
That unitedly we will do the best we can.

To the children of tomorrow, be brave.
Be brave to carry on this massive fight.
So that together, we may fix our broken home,
So that we may restore the world as intended.

48. ALOHA...!

The sun comes up, a new day has begun.
A ray of light slipping through the curtains,
Highlights your face just perfectly.
I lay still, so still, afraid I'd wake you up

I wake up to this beautiful sight and wonder,
When did my life become like a fairytale?
I'd grow up listening to all these folklores.
Little did I knew I'd see it come true.

I had spent most of my life believing,
Stories are just stories, they aren't real.
No one can simply waltz in and change life.
And yet here I am glaring at my biggest truth.

No, I didn't feel butterflies in my stomach,
Nor did I hear any sort of music in the air.
The sky was the same blue, the sun unchanged.
But somehow my whole world was now different.

If only I knew back then I would one day meet you,
That I'd finally know what it's like to feel complete,
That my life would be this magical and beautiful,
I would rush ahead to the day we first said hello.

49. UNSCRAMBLED THOUGHTS

Lately I've felt unattached and lost.
Lost in my head, lost in my thoughts.
Like in a quicksand, sinking slowly.
The more I struggle the deeper I get.

The days have gotten longer and quieter.
I've never really been good at being alone.
My mind always wandering, always busy.
Always echoing countless thoughts untold.

Sometimes I wish there was a reset button.
Maybe it would be good going back in time.
I'd go back to my last moment of pure joy.
But how far behind would that really be?

Or maybe I could skip all these hours
I'd skip all these daunting days.
How much time would I end up losing?
A few days, few months or one too many years?

If it were only possible to time travel.
These options do seem rather tempting.
To be able to alter moments like that.
Would it be worth the big risk?

As I look back at my life so far,
How can I let go of these treasured moments?
These memories I hold close to my heart,
Keep me grounded, keep me going.

As I manage to calm my active mind,
I roll up my sleeves and pick up my baggage.
Slowly but steadily I'll gather myself.
One day I will have it all, I will have it all.

50. I Will Always Love You

Love is patient, love is kind.
When I think of love, you're on my mind.
Love knows no evil, it gives no pain.
It stops you from going insane.
Love brings life, love gives light.
It holds no grudge, it has no fight.
I never knew love, until I knew you
I knew you, the true you.
You never let me stumble, never let me fall.
You gave me more than love,
you gave me your all.
In times of darkness, you were my candle.
There has never been anything you couldn't handle.
I'll always be grateful,
I'll always stay true,
I'll always know love,
'cause I'll always love you.